I0192844

miracles
of the BloG:
A series

Poems by
Carolyn Srygley-Moore

Punk ✦Hostage ✦Press

miracles of the Blog: A series
Carolyn Srygley-Moore

© Carolyn Srygley-Moore 2012

ISBN 978-0-9851293-5-4

Punk Hostage Press
P.O. Box 1869
Hollywood CA 90078
www.punkhostagepress.com

Editor:
A. Razor

Introduction:
Dom Gabrielli

Cover Design:
Geoff Melville

Cover Art Work:
Carolyn Srygley-Moore

Front Cover: *A Girl In A Black Dress* (2012)
Back Cover: *Trapped In A Dollhouse* (2012)

Editor's Acknowledgements

When we speak of extraordinary things in our lives, we tend to use the word "miracle" over and over again.

The word can lose the meaning it was originally intended to have when this is done. For many, though, just being alive, day to day, is a miracle in itself, so the word can never be overused or overlooked. Carolyn Srygley-Moore's writing speaks to the latter aspect in that it voices the emotional state in flux, at the pivotal turning point it is necessary to experience in order to keep on going, live some more, without shrinking away from truth one bit.

It is in this style that all these 'miracles of the BloG' have been written. The style that she has made her own and developed over time in order to communicate the nature of existence along the spiritual demarcations of soul as it is felt from the inside of the author's depths as she bears witness to her truth against the backdrop of the outer world she inhabits with the rest of us.

In essence, these pieces become soul communications, sent along the mental telegraph of spirit in a reflexive voice that bends against the onslaught of life as it cascades over us, but never breaks, miraculously. In as much as this names it's host as you read it, accepting the invitation, this dances away with the reader's heart as well, returning after the pirouette of thought has been completed.

The author was a pleasure to work with, as I feel the playful nature of this book will attest to. All of us at Punk Hostage Press hope this book becomes an enriching poetic experience for you. I could not have done this editing job and the final publishing without the help and support of my partner and the co-founder of Punk Hostage Press, Iris Berry.

I would also like to thank all those that make the press the enterprise it is. Geoff Melville for his work on the cover design and art direction. Lee McGrevin for all the technical support and physical labor he has given. Michele MacDannold and Kimberly Kim for all the work they have done on promotional and coordinating efforts. Danny Baker, for being our first author, S.A. Griffin for being a great mentor, Luis J. Rodriguez for the guidance and inspiration since the beginning, Richard Modiano for the steady encouragement and executive input. Naima Steiner for being the cornerstone of love that gives my foundation it's strength.
C.V. Auchterlonie, Rich Ferguson, Pleasant Gehman,
Joe Donnelly, Jack Grisham, Yvonne De la Vega, Sonny Giordano, Diana Rose, Debbie Kirk,
Frank Reardon, Eduardo Jones, Puma Perl, John Dorsey, Dennis and Annette Cruz and all the other writer's who are part of, or will belong to, the Punk Hostage Press Family, now and in the future.
It takes a lot of folks to keep this press going and growing, we love you all.

Once again, we want to thank the author and artist, Carolyn Srygley-Moore, for her original artwork that are used on the cover design, as well as her wordsmithing, Also our appreciation for Dom Gabrielli and his movingly insightful introduction for this book.

It is all a miracle to behold.

A. Razor
November 2012

Introduction

Violins play. They emanate from distant lands and yet, as we listen to them, they become our intimate thoughts. Poets, Neruda say, become mouthpieces for our loves and we lay with them as we speak them, as we recite them to our loved ones. Their books speak to the intimate, and therefore, the most unknown continents of our singular and vast souls.

Sometimes there are dancers, sometimes there are criminals. Sometimes we are incarnated in both, because we are poets and we speak to the innermost, to the outermost, from the unknown in us and around us.

The emotion that I sense in Carolyn Srygley-Moore's work mingles and flows from all of the above. She is the quintessential poet. Everything that lives in and around her becomes poetry. There are no unturned stones. Everything is hurt and everything could become joy. Strangely no introspection. Carolyn does not stare at things but rather things stir within her. She is a cannibal of objects, a sorcerer of transformations. Hence the Miracles.

Yes, everything is a miracle, because I am still alive. I do not say I am re-born, but I am certainly un-dead. Everything Carolyn writes comes from this victorious stance. Tell me why? Because there are certain so-called illnesses which only have un-repeatable names because there are no cures, no arrangments of their symptoms to create coherence, nebulae of nonsense. Their names are floating between what reality lost and sense has yet to understand. In truth, here one can fall and lose everything. Here the criminals roam, the ones who really hurt, day in day out, with punches in the bosom of freedom, those who imprison, who rape and kill. Can they realize: "When we kill others we are really slaughtering ourselves" ? Doubtful because they must make others suffer to earn their sick enjoyments. Can you be killed and survive? There's one miracle! Trust Carolyn's poems, trust me, a new light will shine. Do not read them, paint them on your living room walls. Understanding is a long process and "we have tamed the monsters," and our "nightmares have died as birds die/ as deer struck by headlights..." Because "I have the tools to restore   to resuscitate/ the wounded/ as never before."

Carolyn's language is locked in capsules, segments of poems sit with images, bright and enigmatic or dark and incomprehensible. Her poems are often aphoristic, lying on the hymen between sense and non-sense. "As God is amorphous   the body lies/ in wait   a tiger's nervous simulacrum." To read 'MIRACLES' is to be invited to a "picnic amongst the graves," where "Lilies migrate like geese   to another Easter." There is something marvelous in every one of Carolyn's poems. Every book must be read, memorized and loved, only then can we do justice to this remarkable writer.

In this afterlife of everyday miracles, where much is still left unsaid; in these tales of ordinary madness where a body has lived 80 moments of night and day; in these tales of timid redemptions, where doubt rivals its sister certainty; in these difficult images, where simplicity often shines like a ruby in dawn silvers, the many graceful faces of Carolyn Srygley-Moore smile. Here in her world of uncountable intellectual and emotional exuberance, the commonplace rises to the sublime, in moments of cherished divinity.

- Dom Gabrielli 2012

6

Dedication

This book is dedicated to all women and men struggling with violence induced PTSD, to say it is indeed possible to overcome it.

It is dedicated to those persons living with bipolar I.

This book is dedicated to my mother, a fiercely loving woman.

It is dedicated to my father who is one of my muses, despite our tragic relationship.

It is dedicated to my stepfather, a good man.

It is dedicated to Evy, the pitbull, white, white.

I would like to extend sincerest love to my brothers, who put up with me as we grew up. Especially my brother John, for his encouragement.

I would like to hug & hold my husband and daughter, who put up with me now.

My friends, Loring Wirbel and David LaBounty, for being there.

Especially my friend Aad De Gids, my best friend.

I would also like to thank foremost God, and the moments when I know redemption is a possibility, a thought which saves me, recklessly, joyfully.

Thank you to A Razor and Iris Berry of Punk Hostage Press for working with me on making this book a living creature, almost, I can almost hear it breathe.

Thank you to Dom Gabrielli, a poet whose work I hold with reverence, for the generous introduction. He makes me see my work in new ways.

And cheers to my people on Facebook.

And cheers to those who have taken a chance and published me over the past twenty years.

And cheers to the trees and my yellow house with the bicycle leaning against the wall in the hush of Milosz, Breton, Derrida, St John, Joris, and all the writers who stir me as if I am a cauldron by which good things might come.

Carolyn Srygley-Moore

November 15, 2012

Ballston Spa, NY

Table of Contents

II. LOVE POEMS

III. PLACE POEMS

IV. Prologue: alternatives to death

*"Those who dive beneath the surface
     do so at their peril."*
     – Oscar Wilde

"I longed to know the world's name."
-- Robert Penn Warren

PRELUDE:
a surveyor's overview

Miracles on York Road

Years past   the domestic violence vigil
poetry was read   music was played   people floated
midair   bearing luminaries   bags of sand fitted with lit
white candles.
*

We walked the streets in   perfect silence
as if a rock star had been murdered   or Vietnam
was suddenly acquiring its due.
*

On the way home we ran over a cat
& took it to the emergency clinic   it could not be
revived.
*

Leave the wounded behind   a man once told me
from behind a desk.   I was filled with bruises.
All deaths are neither painful nor painless   but a drifting
*

as Arabian noon suns spangle.
We walked the streets.   The banshee wailed
brutality is not necessary: beauty is
*

more essential than detail.
The gravel pit is laden with flowers.
Even the spiteful are soothed by fragrant oils
the ground scent   of lavender.

II. A CHILD'S BABBLE

Miracles of a child's babble

It's not supposed to make sense   I say.
Who cares what the facts were?   Trees stood
like guardian vigilantes   observing all.
*

Is it supposed to be child's babble
the white burst at the hairline   almost breathing
nonsense into the past.
*

I sing. I always sing.
I understand the strangest things.
The carnival is a thing of laughter's bone.
*

They say he was anti-Muslim   I say
What Islam is there in Norway?
We know nothing.
*

Skinned night   flayed light.
There is a pause.   My blood is corrupt as anyone's.
As anyone's.

Miracles of a dog's wizardry

The wizard behind the stories
was not shunned   but burnt
at the stake.
*

At twilight the dogs bark
cleaving sunsets
to voice disrepair.
*

My dog is no wizard
but come thunderstorm   lies beneath the desk
at my painted feet.
*

The wizard was not burnt
at the stake
but merely shunned.
*

We aren't to dabble in the black arts
he says. I knew a boy
who dabbled   & his spirit was displaced
*

he dropped out of school
& wrote to me
much later.
*

My dog barks at phantoms.
The god of thunder
has it in for him.
*

He has muscular degeneration
in his skull   his right ear lining
has been removed
*

but neither fact has effected
his capacity
to be afraid

Miracles of a sketched madness

What is madness?   doing the same thing over & over
again expecting a different result   thinking the same
thing.   You are crazy he says   you sound crazy.
*

I bring her plums & ginger-ale.
I bring her white lace dresses for Hawaii
I bring her braces for her bad foot.
*

I hear them arguing my worth
from miles & miles away
the next street over   the next street down.
*

It is a basic disagreement.
She despises crows. Calls them whore cunt skank.
I love crows.
They walk the street as I have wanted to walk the street.
*

You must find a different way of thinking about it   he
says.   It is just a job.   I will bring her plums
& white lace dresses   from the bodies of women
managing survival.
*

You are crazy he says you sound crazy.
I have heard voices since I was nine. I have always been
a stranger. I understand   the stranger of Camus
*

as some cannot.
As some can.

Miracles of Eleanor & Di

I have torn at my face   I have shredded mirrors with
bitten unpainted nails I have guessed
I am more than ageless.
*

There are only so many times
I can describe the coronal burst of the sunset
or the veins just beneath the skin.
*

The dogs have had their supper now.
I am waiting the return of children   the sobbing of
children mostly happy.
*

Silences die a tragic death.
The autopsy discloses more than suffocation discloses
virulent things done to the body.
*

"Eleanor never wanted to live in the White House"
I read in the pages of verity.
Somehow I do not doubt that it's so.
*

Nor did Di ever want to be a princess
puking in the bathroom
living on fish & soup.
*

The dogs have had their supper now. It is hot here.
Humid as an airport
broken open   as the blades of planes
*

spinning from the last century.
The movie To Sir with Love waits for me: I like how he
says "slut"
*

with love. Looking hard into the future.
Looking past the past.
Looking.

Miracles of Eureka in a parallel world

My reading glasses vanish   the page breaks open
hatchling: a child who has disowned God   looks
when tripping on dissolved paper   in the mirror
& realizes behind his threaded ribs
*

lies scaffolding   of soul   spirit   l'esprit
as Poe understood it. Eureka.
In a parallel world   he sees himself:
sees his dead mother's face
*

on the roiling surfaced wind:
sees fluorescent insects appear
as one scrapes the wet sand away from the tier
where a girl with a wooden flute painted crimson
*

plays. Eureka! Day is not night
but for in echo   day is not night
but for in echo.   The shell of the words
*

breaks over the painted   granite page like inhaled
acid rain pounding down upon the teal parallel sea.

Miracles of fear & silence & bicycles
(after a poem by Philip Schultz)

The guard at the Social Security Office wears a Marilyn
Monroe smeared lipstick grin.   The grin of clowns
who are lawyers.
*

Does Zen really practice the virtue of vanishing
as when the war approaches
like a lover's fist?
*

At my daughter's age   what did I fear?
I would squeeze shut my eyes & bicycle into the road
steeped with poisonous berries.
*

I would eat the berries   not knowing
for certain if they were
poisonous.
*

Silence is like that.   Discovering you are
crippled   is like that.
Nobody to blame but the war
*

without agent orange
without agents
without designated victims.
*

I just read a poem by Philip Schultz.
It is a poem about weakness.
Flip the card   is the mantra of fortitude
*

the irreparable mantra   wincing
of strength.

Miracles of fire at core

Foreboding   what will occur.
Hours spent caring for the ungrateful.
& what would gratitude mean. An ember, outed?
*

Go back to sleep   the dogs say.
Fire is the core of the earth
fire is the core of the human being.
*

What is that Marley song   about apartheid?
Before the system   was banished?
About Steven Biko's murder...."you cannot put out a fire."
*

Strange how   one feels a prisoner. Separate.
Strange how   riotous one feels
within the village streets of one's own body.
Setting fires to brush...
*

What would gratitude mean.
Nothing, perhaps. The walls are midwifed
by the fire within them   the dark fire within.
*

Go back to sleep
the dogs say.

Miracles of going into hiding

Going into hiding after being declared
innocent: a hot pink t shirt & sneakers
one body in the ground.
*

& in the prison cells
one can read the holy bible & Camus intermittently
read about driving cars off the edge
*

of accountability.
How many times can one kill
how many times can one be nearly killed
*

without feathers falling upon
the body   from the body   feathers
falling?
*

We die alone a friend says.
We live alone   I say   kneeling on the carpet
praying for the phone to ring.
*

I have gone into hiding at the Y
escorted by nothing   but voices
& a cup of coffee   & reruns of The Prisoner.
*

Which prison is more preferable
the butterflies find their way in & out
I slept like Genet   a lady of the flowers
*

convicted of stealing
a loaf of time.

Miracles of knowing why Heath could not Sleep

Like something out of the Dark Knight I say
no wonder Heath could not sleep
no wonder. I am weeping.
*

We were outside beneath the trees I say
talking & suddenly you walked in
the bank   without saying anything. I looked in the window.
*

There was a man with a gun to somebody's head.
I ran   the next shop down   the next seeking help
they were all being held up: automatics
*

everywhere. By the green dumpster
strangers were gathered   heads down
what is going on I say   my friend
*

went inside the bank.
I knew what you'd do. With few words like a horseman
from a spaghetti western
*

you'd tap the man holding the automatic tap tap
on his shoulder as a child might   playing
to confuse
*

yet not with a child's intent.   There are noises
of sticks breaking loudly of windows
collapsing   of lungs stilled. Guns.
*

Of course of course when I needed you most
you chose to save the world.
Of course.
*

It was a just a dream   my husband says.
Not really I say.
Not really.

Miracles of anti-terror: let's see the damned movie·

If we don't go to the movie
if we sit back on our haunches   like bloodhounds
waiting to feed
we let terror win.

If we sit on our plastic white shower chairs
amidst the clutter of the front porch   & say nothing
as the children scream in a pitch the hounds can hear
        we let terror win.

If we do not page carefully through the sketch pad
sent by the man in violent turmoil   with its pencil
stick figure bodies
falling: if we leave it like a pebble in the mailroom:
        we let terror win.

O hell is everywhere.   There are veins in hell
as there are veins in paradise
able to be cut like summer flowers.

Darling put on that little black dress (burn the orange
wig)   light up a nonfilter cigarette   let us go to
see Batman
        in his last, inglorious   role.

Miracles of the artist's call, says Krapp in his final tape

I am eating a green banana
like Krapp in the last tape   envisioning a boat, death
its engine
cradling the eye-gleam cadenced of my lover.

The world is wrong   I say:
they stopped showing the movie   because it made
no money
because people were fearful of entering the theater
because people were fearful of being seen.

What are we, idiots   I say to the recorder
wary as hyenas beware of lions
wary of doing as the artist calls?

I am going to write something without social
importance.
I am going to write about Christmas trees in August
or the arsonist's light, flaring
or the cadenced eye-gleam of my lover.

But I lapse.   Has evil won
has terror won   a boy with blurred green eyes
that look awry
won?

30

I am gnawing the flesh of a green banana
it is not how they eat them in South America
it is not how they eat them at all: these are not the drug
pins of Columbia
        it is not like that at all.

Miracles of melting highways

The highways are melting.
All women at once remove their makeup.
Our skin is porous in garish light.
*

Highways, melting.   The arteries
buckling beneath the weight of trucks & cars & trucks
bearing cars   to the edge of the brine sea.
*

Such stillness the wind-chimes make no noise.
We dance as such   to the lack of noise.
We have no choice.
*

I have been trapped in a cellar   never tied.
The floor was furnace red.   The walls, white
as shark's teeth dangling from the neck.
*

It was chilled down there.   Can you hear me best
when I speak from the stance of health
or the stance of heat?
*

Everybody hates their parents I read somewhere. I read
there is one in every household:
one like me: locked by choice.
*

Highways.   One could throw oneself before a truck but
mutilation is no option. The casket must be
open   for the kiss goodbye.
*

For the nickel on the eyelid
that keeps the lid shut
that keeps the intent on elsewhere
*

like the star dial
& the stuffed cat
in the pharaoh's tomb.

Miracles of painting the ash pink

What is beauty   in the eyes of the Taliban?
I would go & paint murals the size of elephants
on the streets of their abode
*

but war is as factual as beauty seems.
Executions in the town square:
Sun gleams on the round faces watching.
*

I once worked at a pizza parlor
& a boy told me how easy it is to strangle a chicken
he took me through it step by step.
*

I see no chickens
but in my friend Beth's henhouse
the eggs piled in a blue bowl upon her blue counter.
*

My daughter grew up on a farm   my friend says.
She knows what the facts of life are.
I hope not.   I wonder.
*

Beauty is a strange thing.
I would paint the ash of the dead pink
if I had the means.

Miracles of Penicillin

The mouth   pink
pains from kissing chewing devouring pronged starlight
the fierce constellations one by one.   History.

Ancient stories fleshed muscle of tongue peels & arches.
*

Penicillin is an old story.
Take with food or water.   Saved how many lives
over course of hours; stopped plagues   purpose

revealed accidentally like the structure of carbon.
*

You go off with the dog for a drive.
Our instincts are   to pass along what we know
is true   as if talking to the dead about their past lives

will help matters.
*

We walk the pale blue bottom of an emptied swimming
pool   dodging the dead creatures the squirrel the bird
the toad.   We are careful as people living with HIV

fearful of contagion.   One cell displaced malingers.
  *

I take my dose of penicillin. The tablets are white.
Now they say the Mickey Mouse from the carnival
may be a pedophile.

There is no sanctity.
*

The woman in the painting
over the fireplace   appears made of glass.
The glass changes color like water.

As the flesh changes
*

as God to you & I are different things.   I believe in the
variable.   We don't talk about it   anymore.
The gulf between us is reds & browns.

We should keep shut   our broken mouths.

Miracles of people in paintings by rivers

We are each a character in a painting
or an object   (water lilies on the grand murals) the
woman enacting the St Vitas dance
in Breughel's vista of the dark ages.

We live in big houses or shacks
down by rivers   in sketches on the family wall
led to during drunken outbursts:
this is the painting we took from the building by the river
as the house of our history burnt down.

I inhabit for a moment the sketches of Michelangelo
I am a man ink & charcoal   utter perfection   formed
I have cast the woman aside   with a kind of mercy
a kind of sorrow.

I return   a woman in proper blue bearing a paper
parasol by the waters of Renoir
laughing   or regressed to the child
bearing the flowers.

Or a naked woman with no ribs visible: I have never
heard of Jesus   I am
bearing mangoes for Gaughin's black teeth   grinding
after the sweating work is done
& my hands are filthy.

Miracles of rabbit pelts promised

Hands hard on my back   he'd sing
Bye O Baby Bunting   Daddy's Gone A-Hunting.
The rabbit pelt promised was soft on my skin.
*

Some people weep   for themselves only.
A hero is assassinated   buildings fall   planes are
diverted: they weep for themselves alone.
*

He was like that.
All his voices clamoring at once   for release:
he should have been an artist
*

painting the piece   where the house burnt down. The
rabbit pelt sang.
I get letters now from cousins telling me
*

how fond they were   of him.
Strange.   He showed greater kindness to strangers
like a character in a Williams play.
*

The sun is silent now   a sluiced artery.
A man is weeping beside the green dumpster.
He is weeping for the world.
*

He is even weeping   a little   for me.
His fists are blocking his eyes, scrounging for vision   or
water.   He is hungry but not in a violent way.

Miracles of refuting definition

Never to return or refute that day.
Passed out on the floor.
Never to recapture. Never to be captured.
*

Double slashes mark the clouds
I have abandoned them   I choose spaces instead
*

a kind of pacing within the body.
            Never to return   that day
screaming like the Talking Heads: what have I done!
*

Nothing lies beneath the shirtsleeves rolled up
nothing able to be violated.
*

Double slashes   are aggressive
            I am awash with nothingness
as by warm milk straight from the goat's teat.
*

I will not be captured.   She sings
                I am neither pagan nor Christian
I am neither straight nor gay.   I refute definition
*

she sings   from the windowsill
        sings to the ears of the physicians   who choose
physics over love.
*

Double   gash sutured.
We transcend the confines of our own bodies. Never to
be defined
*

as a painter forsakes his brush strokes
the translucent gauze skirt   the opiate that is water.
The space   used   in use redefined.

Miracles of sleep's refusal

Sleep refuses me like a lover
kicks me away   pummels my breasts   a boxer
taking a stance.
*

Cup-stacker   player of legerdemain
sleep is no poison.   Hell is devoured
by petals of orange.
*

Dogs are the dominant miracle.
As I walk them I spot the geese preparing for a return
to the sun   although it is out of season.
*

I am the invisible one.
I paint self-portraits of fluted blues
that sound-out into nothingness.
*

I am the sad one. In the car I speak loudly
as if speaking to a creature on the other side of the
windshield & the passengers plug their ears.
*

I am the joyful one. In chorus I sing solo.
I am thin as the cello's bow
played on a Baltimore rooftop one early spring
*

as a woman reads of Malte's death
the kernel of death   that roots inward.
Sleep refuses her too   like a lover.

Miracles of surviving the age 27

Twenty seven is a harsh age.
Joplin died then. Cobain.   Winehouse. The sky
is a butcher   time is no thief but heroin may be.
*

I see her standing alone on a field of ice
without blood now
without blood to betray her.
*

The flesh peeled back   like an avocado
the muscle in mounds glistening
there is no blood.
*

I am told when you do heroin you piss yourself.
You flail against the door   & piss yourself.
You cannot see the sun.
*

The Updates are unconfirmed.
She was in her own home   a good thing.
A photograph perhaps   as she fell
*

held her eyes for an instant.
Not the Grammy.   Outside, London
passed by   draped in reds & grays.
*

Someone found the body.
Someone always finds the body.
They will feel that cold   unyielding   for years.

Miracles of the abandoned train trestle

On the abandoned train trestle I came upon a man like a
blind woman approaching windows.
He said: your dog is fat.
*

We are from Florida.
My dog's soul is radiant as a child
from her first kick in the sea.
*

I like fat dogs   he said.
Mosquitoes & gnats on the trestle settle on the wound
stretched on the smile between us.
*

I understand.   He is climbing the village streets
looking down impasses
seeking avenues.
*

I understand. The wound between us
dances & flirts & is a union
geographically speaking.
*

Is the soul ever born violent?
I feel happy   as I ever have.   The stranger departs,
smiling calmly.
*

Time stretches its wound before me.
I decide to leave it without sutures.
I decide to let it be.

Miracles of the Evening News

The historian was arrested:
peers from the prison window   upon a floodlight
spiraling over the bloodhound grounds.
*

In small gunpowder outbursts
we measure our time
watching someone come up the back walk with a bundle
of rage.
*

The historian focused upon presidents
like a boy lost   walking home alone for the first time
counting out sidewalk panes by rote.
*

What does it feel like to be suffocated?
It must feel like a game at first
it must feel like play.
*

A few weeks ago   the shuttle took flight
a flare of blue & orange   like a great tiger lily
advancing against the night.
*

Neruda was an old lover   I tell a friend:
we slept together for years
in the print of tiger paws.

Miracles of the fiction in the glass

When we kill ourselves
who are we really killing   the fiction in the glass
the shape caught through the eye's corner
walking past Broadway
*

Shop fronts? We zip the red lace lingerie
for our meeting with God   we unzip the jeans
we unzip what we wear   traversing the urban streets.
*

Everything is not a haiku   someone said.
Pink hues in the trees cast by the camera.
When we kill ourselves
*

is it what we despise?   Or what we love
that we endeavor to destroy.   When we kill others
are we really slaughtering our selves.
*

I woke up laughing this morning.
My daughter was home   her face tanned & fuller.
I wrote of the dead   was filled with the fact
*

that I am not dead. Not yet. Two near death
experiences wasted me.   Planted me like pink
swastikas before the Nazis altered   their symbolism:
once a symbol
*

of origin   not evil.
There are so many dead people   my brother said
as he passed a graveyard on the path to the marina.
*

Can we have a picnic amongst the graves   I asked.
No   my mother said.   Leave the dead
to their own devices. Leave the dead   to their own.

Miracles of the I as a limitless pronoun // a treatise
of sorts

Do I talk about myself too much I once said to a friend;
what do we know better   than ourselves he said.
A Yale scholar, I believed him.

Kidnapped babies found dead or alive
congenital searches:
& the   austere headlines fall away
*

necessarily.   We talked the world. If you think I am
speaking of myself   you are mistaken.
The I is not a limited pronoun.   It exists within
realms of imagination.
*

This is a story told atop   a rocky blue hillside
overlooking a city   once of importance in
the industrial world.

It is no longer of importance. It is a pebble trembling
like brine foam in a paper cup.
*

This is a story told   by a woman
who has not had her coffee yet   who feels
like a pulsing neon alien in a concrete urban landscape.
*

A woman once invited my mother over to her home
for coffee in order to decipher for herself what daughter
she had versus the daughter my mother had raised.

Complicit parties:
*

rebels smoking joints   behind the church &
schoolyard.   If you think I am speaking of myself
you are mistaken.

But the self even cast aside forms   amorphous
*

essential as the headlines
necessary as the pelvis joined to the spine
necessary as any hinged   or unhinged bone.

Miracles of the migrating lily *(for Jack Varnell)*

The old bell, the husk of a bell   sounds
in the tower like   a child's cry.
I don't want to grow up   she wails.
*

Lilies migrate like geese
to another solvent Easter.
Love is unlike ecstasy   the tablet: you can't spit it
before dissolved.
*

Skin changes as the sky changes.
As God is amorphous   the body lies
in wait   a tiger's nervous simulacrum.
*

Summer tumbles its tubular
straws through which focus is sucked
brain damage of sorts.
*

I am tired of thinking about death.
I am tired of thinking about life.
Color lies in wait   in between.
*

Bones sing from the windowsill.
Femur rib tibia phalange   sing.
Some say the human is not an animal: I disagree.
*

Living at the Y
I saw the animal in the human.
The shelters are
*

more dangerous than the street.
A blue halo reconstructs itself   like hip or lung.
It belongs to anyone.

Miracles of the refrain

Watching   as from a distance: this is how
I am going to die   is the refrain
amidst repeated Jesus Christ's.
*

& sometimes   you do die. Not global jihad.
A gunman with blue eyes arrives   & shoots the place
up.   Oklahoma City in Norway.
*

Too bad   madness takes such forms.
The solar system
is wired.
*

I am going to talk about myself   briefly.
At those occasions when I should have feared for myself
I did not.   I was that crazed.
*

On the train you can see trees pass
with features in the trunks   as I would sketch bark
fastidiously   when a child.
*

& sometimes you do die.
The people left do not know   how to balance
the checkbook.   They'll figure it out.
*

It's not "I wish you were here"
but I wish you   forever.

Miracles of the whispered microphone

The singer whispers into the microphone
& does not sing.   Shadows of death's blue tattoos
pass over the face   there is no song.
*

The word is never.   The tabloids repeat it
eating themselves like grains of salt   as the animal
cleans itself   salt of which they are comprised.
*

I was not there when my father died.
They found the body   half-in half-out a doorway
but I wept from six hundred miles away.
*

What do we weep for   when the passing ensues?
What could have been   but never was;
what was?
*

Everyone has the void   my friend says.
Not the void one stares-down like a cat's green eyes
but the void that teeths us   gnaws   like a baby's
rattler inside.
*

I am no singer. I never whispered into a microphone.
I hissed like the snake charmer's snake
under somebody else's direction.   The flute was
green.
*

Ecstasy is a bad pill. Rather
falling   to glide along the desert sands, our stomachs
bare   glide
the fields of salt   the gathered grains of salt.
*

The tabloids say nothing   of novelty
concerning the dead or the living.
Green tattoos of desertion   a circus of implication.

Miracles of the moving trees

Uncertain? No. I have my dogs
I have seen the trees move
hence   I have seen the wind
*

hidden   in my sock drawer. It appeared blue
as the corridors of time.
*

A mathematical principle.
What we see written on the underside of the bridge what
names of the dead are hence written?
*

I have witnessed the motion
grass   leaves   tumbling & carried
not by virtue of their own strength.
*

Uncertain? No.
The world maintains a deaf heart.
The discourse is important: woman as Eve or
*

woman as a defunct whore? It is not all or nothing. There
are many faces   to the human spirit.
What name we see written on the belly
*

of the metro   we lie on the tracks   as it passes
through our very cells   carried by the wind.
The most certain wind.

II. LOVE POEMS

Miracle of Sunglasses

The city of nightmare roads wound tight as the seeds of
figs   & people I did not know or understand
ran naked through the streets blue   as uncut veins.

Somebody cried my name. It was some sort of game
where trees were hungry for the blood of nests built in
their armpits with paper & weed.

O it was in the mountains that love first lay me down. I
drank no wine. Sober as a toothpick & opened
for the boy who could not read   who wept, needing.

You do not know enough to draw a Rembrandt in love
the official said;   you are gathering spore
you are in wait for story after story.

& Why do you talk about God when you do not think
about God?   What do you talk about gardens
when you are no gardener?

Baltimore is the perfect juncture for self destruction
I told a man   seated around a watering hole
in the wintry desert.

I have lived origins as I have lived sparcity.
The man's hand touched the curve of my belly. I wore
my sunglasses for self-protection.

He left next morning, with no goodbye.

Miracles of summer in the rearview mirror

Lost the new watch with the blue striped band
the color of a boat's sail   & it bloomed out with air
like a used tire   even when the wind was still.

I taught a child   how to dive
though I don't know how to dive   simply know
how to go headfirst in water   arms pinned over my
ears....

I learned to love
the night shift   leaning back into the loom of the lost
clock   the wristwatch dangling on a ceiling somewhere
almost melting, silvery   extracted like bone from a
Dali painting.

Dogs entered the home
dogs exited the home   jumping upon bandits
their faces painted like velvet raccoons   ditched dogs
like pitbull   puppies   saved.

I took a new name
& forsook another name   displacing diseases
with the count of white lily petals   descending to the
core of Heaven & Hell.

Love was near. Love was always near.
My daughter cleaned her room like the inside of an
upright piano. I bribed her.   She whistled to me
& I knew she taught herself   how to dive
as I once taught her   to breathe.

Miracles of bird watching with Hitchcock

We have watched each other disappear
through birdwatcher binoculars   traced the crow
feather dropped
against the biblical text   of the elements.
*

We have watched each other return
placed the anchored binoculars on the windowsill
for instruments were of no necessity.
*

The rings around Saturn are fantasy
As the ring on my finger   as my body molts
its lungs of desire.
*

They fall to the wayside. It has nothing to do
with luck   this fear of falling
this fear of flying.
*

Hold onto me now, love
the elephant kneels gracefully   only before beauty
which exists: she kneels before us.
*

I hold onto you.   We smell like monsters.
We have tamed the monster.
We are linked by fallibility   by the fact
*

that there is much we cannot do.   A black bug scuttles
under the refrigerator.   Probably harmless
you say.   I cling to that. I cling.
*

The terror is gone.
Hitchcock made his appearance   climbing aboard a
yellow bus.   It is a good thing.

Miracles of cartoon realisms

You love cartoons.   We talk those of our childhood:
televisions we woke to early cold Saturday mornings to
lie prone on our stomachs   watching Rocky &
Bullwinkle   in black & white
*

or the bird running across the screen
through hill & valley   running
to nowhere   a kind of immortality.
*

I met someone who jumped off a Baltimore roof.
She ate Mickey Mouse & thought she could fly
or if not fly vanish   off the chart like Roadrunner.
*

Or come back from her demise
in an instant   by virtual wisdom
of flipping the channel   or the animator's sketchbook
wish.
*

She was half-maimed
with nervous pockmarked hands
& told me   ma'am I could not fly.
*

The dust rises in clouds like biblical locusts
once the one who is running meets fate.
The clouds were gray
*

as the walls of the living room
& that white sofa the dog would furtively lie upon
when mother was not watching.
*

The young German Shepherd watched cartoons with me
panting   as if in symbiosis
with the one pursued.

Miracles of dancing dogs

We talk about it:
the incidents in Tennessee.   I should never have
let you go   you say.
Never second-guess your own mothering I say.
*

It is good we came to terms   with the skyscape
of our own accord it is good we were not told what to
think: it is good.
*

Love or freedom   I hear my husband singing
downstairs as the dogs dance for bread.
It is his birthday.
*

How to love   through the pain of it.
It hurt.   There was no brain damage
*

to speak of.
The horizon has its own laws.
It is jagged yet serene. It is an ellipsis & a period.
*

Love or freedom. The vegetarian chili simmers
on the stove.   We are deplete of chili powder.
We will make do
*

We have learned to make do.
He still has nightmares. My nightmares
have died   as birds die
*

as deer are struck   by headlights
along the spooling road
as the metal truck of joy   crushes terror's vagrant ribs.

.

Miracles of darkness

I have the tools to resist   your darkness.
I bear stars like torches in my bare hands.
The horse I ride   is not a dark horse.
*

I understand   doing something terrible.
I understand. I have waved my fists to the scalding
dawn   singing   My God what have I done
*

as blood dripped down my thighs.
It was long ago.   I am still capable of
stilly flights   of playing with feathers that are not there.
*

Your darkness is not your war   it is your warrior.
It makes sense to work with the fabric
the thread torn between your teeth since birth:
*

what you are used to.
I try to guide those in need of guidance.
Usually   I fail.   I name the most desperate
*

by birdcall   the calls that are the sweetest
the calls that haunt.   I have the tools to resist your
darkness. I have the tools to restore   to resuscitate
*

the wounded
as never before.

Miracles of elephants & running errands

There is an intimacy   to running errands
together   in glittering black jackets & combat boots
our bodies empty of tattoos
*

but for those garnered by shadows cast
over the sides of our faces.
Have you ever looked an elephant   full
*

in the face   I asked you.
Have you ever read the word elephant
& used the word in your work
*

knowing it was not the same
elephant?   My child & I were driving away
from you   toward other loves
*

discussing the mother elephant's wail when she loses
her young. It is the most ferocious grief
audible to man   I say; yes   she says.
*

She is twelve   yet she comprehends.
On our journey we run errands
say the word elephant
*

the elephant of Hemingway or Valentine or
Animal Planet   changed   in our very mouths.
I have never looked an elephant   full in the face
*

but I have seen memory & grace
twined like grey trunks   between lovers
between   parent & child
*

between   strangers.
Sing it out I say tearing at my hair burning my hair for
grief
*

laying me down
laying me under.

Miracles of Lady Gaga & Jesus

How has magical realism effected
your words she asks; I stammer. In gardening
I do not remember source or certitude.
*

The rhododendron leaves have blackened
leaning in coils against the trunk
which also is leaning   sparse as a cirrus cloud.
*

Did it rain today   I ask
she is leaving for camp tomorrow.
She is starting to think for herself.
*

Lady Gaga & Jesus   tucked under her arm.
Gila monsters in her trunk
in case she must frighten the water away.
*

She had a dream of drowning
when she was three   & told everyone
she had drowned.   She had not, really, drowned
*

but emerged like a sea maiden from the pool
her blond hair plastered to her neck
her mouth an oval   gasping.
*

She knows how to swim now.
She knows how to sing.
I do not recall either source or certitude
*

but in the gash   of the light
in the gash of her birth that nurse
who had survived   Lidice, June, 1942.

Miracles of lettuce

I am exhausted too, swollen
with waiting   the smell of hospital rooms
a man wobbling between hallucination & lucent dream.
*

I clear the roof of wedges of sunlight
as of snow & ice in winter's treachery: why
am I so damned sensitive I say   to the squirrel
*

curled half-alive in the street below me?
Regret occurs as an option
regret occurs.
*

Lettuce is an aphrodesiac   to the ancient Egyptians.
Let us paint our eyes   black
& wander amidst the constellations.
*

Yes   my friends & I   gathered around
a bowl of lettuce   wet with tap water
seeking not genital success   but simplicity of affection.
*

I am tired too.   Each day
brings a different failure.   God walks down the halls
turning off the lights
*

but defeat is no option.
Stupid, stupid me.

Miracles of listening to 80's Alternative while soldiering snow in summer heat

After an afternoon of eating fresh peaches
& sweeping the floors
we head out to select a new door
*

from a wood & fiberglass menagerie
We have not left yet.
The window is still shattered   the print of hand
*

filling void.
The heat bursts through in waves, electric.
Add water & one could die, in voltage
*

unless the breakers triggered.
We are listening to eighties alternative:
she drives me crazy   Joey.   Once in a Lifetime:
*

This was my favorite song   I tell him.
At hospital they would give me hour long leaves
to walk the snow-slung terrain
*

& I would listen to Byrne scream
My God   what have I done
through my yellow walk man
*

& throw up my own hands in consonance
to the upstate sky.
It is still my favorite song.
*

But for the vagaries of Dr Zhivago's
opening strains
where too one soldiered the snow.

Miracles of personal clutter

Everybody heads at once   into the water.
An orchestration almost indecent
elbows like violin bows   veins like strings.
     *

We watched from the shore.
Our eyelashes gathered light like snow.
Our bodies fattened   withered   in moon cycles.
     *

Did we watch as ourselves   or as a couple ;
history withdrew its obligations
history withdrew its embrace.
     *

Personal details lay like clutter
on the sill between
where the magician lay his cards: choose one, he'd say.
     *

We'd choose another.
We watched the people swim   & play their bodies
into an enormous music
     *

we knew surpassed all memory.
The life source shone as wound shines
as petal shines in the rain
     *

once fallen from its axis.
As stone bleeds   in the rain.
     :

Miracles of solitude

Youth runs out of breath like autumn's
flaring reds like a love's departure.
The crow takes to the extinguished embers & devours
them like bread.

Friends, of course. Youth runs
& runs escaping the nightmare's masked man diving
through the window creating
the circle of life with his very body.

Don't leave. We have bread to break
we have monsters to share. My friends are leaving for
Minneapolis the Galapagos for terms of seizure with the
ways of wind.

I am not alone. Not really. I have my dogs
I have memory. I own nobody.
I own a tenth of an acre of land a yellow house.
I own walls that move.

Miracles of spending time at home

When wind is simply solitude
or the dream of a long arm covered with green tattoos
or the yellow dress   born by the bride with parrots
aligned to her shoulders
*

we sit, she & I   & consider home.
We prefer home   not like trappings
or the alternative to adventure
*

but dogs on the torn sofa, nesting
cats on the ottoman.
Entrenched in the green curtains, wind chimes
*

the filigree of wing.
Laundry is like wonder clipped to the vine
the woman of jungle swings.
*

Lies do die, it is so   like bad fictions
sour in the mouth   like sacs filled with dead fetuses
carried before the townspeople   with utter shame.
*

I have known blame.   Still, I am good
at keeping my face on.   I hold it on a stick
a Grecian mask   as somebody sings
chorus to the comedy.
*

Nobody is laughing.   But nobody is weeping, either.
& the corners of the mouth   turn upward, slightly
as if drawn by a greasepaint stub.

Miracles of starting-over

It seemed like   a starting over
the feathers floating on the air   like ships
removed from their bodies   becoming the sea.
*

It seemed like a starting over.
We put the baby in the car-seat   & drove
until bridges were made of dew   not flesh & bone.
*

Particles of dew   like candy wrappers
glistened in the light   brushed the earth
with wishes.
*

We watched people at diners voraciously. Shall we take
new names   we asked   shall we take
pseudonyms?
*

There were ways of acting   we had not understood.
We stood our ground.   The sky
was different   the very constellations changed
*

even the stories
passed down from the ancients
changed.

Miracles of the crowd

In the crowd I see you
as one sees   the bluebell of absence
or a kite   tangled in a tree-line.
*

True we were never lovers.
You bear a paintbrush like Matisse
& lore is your denuded model
*

seated on a chair like a boy.
One can milk stones   for water.
One can milk bones   for bread.
*

In the crowd I see you.
Apparently you cannot stop weeping.
I would like to kiss you on the neck
*

where the hollow is, like a teat.
I would like to see what you bleed.
It is not empathy.   Or is it.
*

The heat is stifling. We don't let our child
walk home alone.
We hold her hands   still.
*

When does danger stop & adventure
begin?   I milk the pebbles
as the kitten   weaned   pummels my chest
*

seeking mother.
I have digressed.
We are blessed with solitude.
*

We are blessed with the vision of banana trees.
There is nothing abstract about it.
We hold on tight.

Miracles of the ghost-kite, rider

It's how some think.
A back-turned reel of a movie.
I never learned how to do the tango   a friend remarks
*

over breakfast.
We granted him refuge   to heal him.
The kite is a ghost-kite, something superlative about it.
*

I write   I write about God all the time
as the fascists look over my shoulder.
I write about God.
*

I hear your voice   clacking in the loom.
A great tapestry is evolving.
Where are you   I ask: you are far away
*

walking the markets of New York LA Rotterdam.
Picking out cantaloupes to please you.
You are no fascist.   You don't care for God
*

much, but tolerate.
I sprinkle Jesus in your coffee, a white powder
similar to cocaine.   The mouth numbs.
*

It is hard to speak at all.
Let's stand here in the light   let's switch off the
darkness   & see what happens.
*

I don't know the tango he says   rather I know
the martial arts   he says.   Put the ghosts in the car &
light it on fire   he says;   there is no point
*

to the ghost-kite, rider.
There is no point.   But learning to dance the tango
a yellow rose in the teeth   is another matter.

Miracles of the tardy handyman

Waiting for the handyman
his belt filled with tools   the ash of construction sites
clinging to his shirtsleeves
*

I want to fix
the body failing   not my own
I want to fix the recurring nightmare
*

the night terrors   the sweats.
The handyman was meant to be here   an hour and a
half ago: I have been waiting with the dogs
*

fashioning lists   of all things in need of fixing.
The fists in the wall need spackled
The molding around the window   was destroyed
*

by an ancient leaking air conditioner.
Bowls of envelopes need tending.
Bowls of the ill-addressed intention
*

the ill-conceived.   I want to fix
the failing bladder legs eyes   the failing brain.
To make it fail that it will not know
*

just what the occasion is.
Birthdays & deaths   are marriage, each.
Fishing-lines cast into the void
*

& drawing forth the catch
The turtle must be   thrown back
that the heart can swim.

Miracles of the toy red sailboat

The heat wave has dissipated.
I am no meteorologist   waving my arms before an
electronic field   I am only a woman who just walked
the dogs.
*

I am avoiding the headlines today:
turn the air conditioner to fan
turn off the overhead lights.
*

There is the noise of water running
as if the house was a river
& I am a boy's toy red sailboat   meandering currents
with covetous bass.
*

The sailboat too has a belly turned upside
to be cut open   gutted   guts filling the colored
Sunday funnies.
*

As a kid I walked in upon my father in the drafty garage
he was preparing the fish for supper.
I found it interesting.   How the funnies bled color
*

& all artifice was abandoned.
The axis is: I am only a sailboat my husband likes to
move gently along the silvery river   with a stick
cleaved
*

from the blue oak of all childhood.
He loves me   he loves me not   is no game I play.
The flower has no petals for counting.
*

The sailboat floats belly-up   like fish or buoy
demarking the zone where danger begins
where affection ends.
*

I am avoiding the headlines   today.
My words incriminate nobody   but myself.
Myself is an approximation   as is the vector
*

the horse & arrow spinning
atop the hex sign barn. I am from the land of
horse & buggy.   I cherish & disparage
*

all origins
as I do with what I have become.

Miracles of the utility room

I hate doing laundry   he writes
I do too   I write   especially the folding.
Our utility room is filled with unfolded clothes
*

spilling over the shelves where the black cats sleep.
Nothing in that room   is intended for flight.
Even the spiders coexist in suspended animation
*

caught in their own webs   the webs they've woven.
Years ago   I was talking to a friend
my daughter ran to me: where do I go to hide
*

from the forces of evil? she screamed.   The utility room
I said.   My friend laughed.
My daughter ran & a door slammed.
*

That door is jammed now   slammed
hard on the fourth of July   it will not open.
My husband took hammer & pliers   to it: still
it refused to open.
*

Nothing in that room   is intended for escape.
The cosmos could change its every root
its every tail & dorsal   fin pinned to the body
*

of all that is good in us
the utility room would remain as-is.   It is upside-down
rich with the forces of evil   seeped-in & banished
*

a vortex where matching socks vanish   red & black:
where cartoon cats sleep like commas   mascots
of what cannot be known   much less defined.

Miracles of trembling

There is a whoosh when the umbilical is cut
An anti-noise   whoosh as of a ghost loosed.
So I have been informed
*

by men in surgical masks with surgeon's hands
hands that are not allowed to tremble.
I blame neither moon nor sun but
*

dew on the grass in wind trembling.
What do we do but follow
nature's intuitions?   Whoosh   another cord
*

is cut.   Another ghost of the past released.
In the fog that swallows the grasses
there is truth.   There is truth.
*

I choose not to watch the news today.
I will ride the tortoise back into the sun
squinting against the dark   my hands, trembling.

Miracles from waking in a Casablanca

.

When I find myself in the movies
I am a prop in Casablanca   the makeup on Ingrid's
face the blacked-out grin in the Nazi's mouth.

The airplane waits on the runway
the tarmac lights glisten on my skull bone
the round of an ocean jetty.

Who is leaving whom? Is this love
the better of the thousand loves I know is this love
the more honorable of a thousand faces?

The game goes on
like water spilling over a waterfall   like the small steps
in the mountainside

carved by rain & snow & simplest acts of pure erosion.

I watch the game, holding hands
with husband & daughter each, holding hands with the
past & the future, gripping tight.

We spill over notches in history though I cannot recall
the highlights in name & date only cause of a kid
eating cheese curls while riding the scarlet waterfall.

Miracles of waking up laughing

I woke up laughing.
My baby is home sleeping   on the couch.
The playful vultures are eluded   now at bay.
*

I woke up to the Video   *Wild, Wild Night.*
I dance to it. I've been told I am
a bad dancer. So what.
*

As I dance I am thinking   I used to hear this daily
when I had no lock & key
when I had no home.
*

Here I am with what I thought would never happen.
The man   watches me dance   smiling.
The child   asleep on the sofa   home.
*

Two dogs.
Is that John Goodman I say   in the video.
There are all sorts of cameos. I love John Goodman.
*

I do not feel hollow   as a chocolate rabbit.
I do not feel hollow   as the feminine principle.
*

I woke up laughing.
I woke up laughing. I have been in a dark place.
Not yesterday.   I remember
*

the lights are bright   & harsh
as one emerges.
Should one choose to emerge.

III. PLACE POEMS

Miracles of Glass Street

In the first miracle there was complete departure from
autobiography   she considered women who were
leaders   their hands trembling like glass lanterns
as the abyssal trains passed.

In the second miracle   the occurrence of death
amazed   the coffins heaped with tons of red roses
spilling over the glass top
for all coffins are made   of glass.

In the third miracle   clocks were stopped
mirrors were turned the other way
there was room for neither time nor reflection.

In the fourth miracle she knew she was pregnant
not with child   but with image   & would bleed for all
her days   for this cycle's reason: as if
she put her belly through a window.

In the fifth miracle glass became trees
trees became voice
voice became her.

In the final miracle   she stopped seeing reflection as
betrayal   she could see the tomboy's face with
the white sailor cap   she could call herself by her
nickname & answer   as glass answers light.

Miracles from Cape Cod

In the first miracle hinges were removed from the shop
galley windows & doors & the sea could be seen
from every perspective a great green dragon
a biblical behemoth a dinosaur coexisting with humans.

In the second miracle she swam with her friend naked
out where the tide was inconsequential draping itself
like God in folds of un-skin.

In the third miracle an older man took her arm on the
sands he took her into the dunes & she fought & cursed
until he let her go tissue most intimate still intact.

In the fourth miracle the engine stalled in her escape
& they pushed the car until it could be pushed no longer
as the blade of fatalism cleaves yet as one is an actor.

In the fifth miracle she smoked a joint with her brother at
the cabin where her parents were staying
thus the paranoia took root like scarlet perennials.

In the final miracle she woke to the sea just outside her
window Ferris Wheels spinning great orange
juggernauts: in ensuing windstorm she came to terms
with being herself.

Miracles from the Garret

The assault of dusk on daylight
is a mind-game   not exactly assault
but ending with full penetration nonetheless.
*

Let me sleep   daylight says
let me sleep.
*

The sublime is dwarfed   by the landscape
dwarfs the landscape   filled with final choices
filled with second chances.
*

Hiding places lie in devastation
in hope   in the garret
from which Frank watched   the war planes
*

& dreamt of kissing Peter.
Let me sleep   daylight says
let me sleep.
*

Chimera is   a favorite word.
History was my favorite subject   until I lost
all sense of time
*

& departed into the future.
I saw it wreck   on the skyline
like any train.
*

Let me sleep   it said
let me sleep.

Miracles in the Street of the Old Schoolhouse

In the first miracle the husband said that place
was a dump   she said was it really   he said you
were out of it then   you were a mess:
I don't remember she said.

In the second miracle she remembered   the time prior
to the daughter   the night of the blizzard winging over
the city   & the sudden call from the payphone by
Cumberland Farms.

In the third miracle the light of existence was not pale
but crimson she locked herself in the bathroom with a
Scout knife   & all sense of autobiography is ended.

In the fourth miracle the police knocked the door down
she was conscious curled in a ball at the foot of the bed
nearly dead   from all-over trembling as a cat trembles
while in labor.

In the fifth miracle she acquired empathy for all creatures
like a character in Deep Space Nine   able to feel the
thoughts of others able to feel   the feelings like
accident, denuded.

In the final miracle all was left   behind the old
schoolhouse   the woman running the length of the
building calling   David please let me in
to Grecian archetypes & seas of doors broken in.

Miracles of Baltimore`

Trapped by the self in the poem he says.
Sometimes one is trapped I say.   In Baltimore I lived
in a studio   iron bars on the windows
*

& listened to the cockroaches nesting
in the hair on my lover's chest.   I read Nietzsche
& Rilke & Wilde   one by one: lemmings pushed
from the harbor's edge
*

by defaced strangers   bearing broomsticks.
Wilde spoke of concealing the artist to reveal art.
Nietzsche spoke of making one's own way.
*

Rilke wrote of Such Things.
Wonder encapsulated in the noise of the playground
beyond vision   for blue bars on the windows.
*

I was beaten only once by a lover.
He left welts on my back & buttocks.   There was pain
there was adrenaline   there was the flight of
the cartoon roadrunner.
*

I left that chamber   of bars on the window.
But I can erect them at will.
as they erect themselves   at will.

Miracles of Birthday Street, the Netherlands *(for Aad)*

In the first miracle lay a celebration of chaos
college students midst snowstorm
tipping over dumpsters & garbage cans   carrying iron
tables from libraries of disrepair.

In the second miracle love was not wanting but satiated
itself in a curl without lust
on a painting by Matisse as his eyes were dying.

In the third miracle   people touched the cloak
the stranger wore it was Johnny Cash or Ashton Nyte or
a Goth   wearing white face paint & black nail
polish upon long pianist hands.

In the fourth miracle   the abyss fell through
the west grasped the Orient & vice versa
there was terror of seas unleashed & yet no fear at all.

In the final miracle   it was somebody's birthday
the dogs piled on the bed in apprehension
chaos filed itself away on the bedside table
beneath certainty.

Miracles of Detour Street *(for my stepdad)*

Clinging to the cliff of avarice
this is no celebration of erasure   we drive seven hours
through detours & warning signals
*

to see one another face to face. We are creatures
of habit: take care of the dogs the house the rabbit
take care of our selves.
*

Sky folds like sunset skin
we are lit by wanting another   to make it through
to make it through.
*

Messages float in on clouds of ether
we wish you strength & prayer be with you. It's not about
me   I say   it is not about me.
*

I can see the nerves like wires beneath my skin;
my daughter takes a pen   & moves the violet vein
pronounced on the back of my hand. Gross she says.
*

The body speaks.
The body speaks.

Miracles of Goth Street

What do I hear in you.
A jazz club   snapped fingers? A room
filled with smoke & mobsters
filled with guns & light?
*

The heart stammers   but grows
to speak in complete sentences
like Darth Vadar in full drag.
*

What do I hear in you. Goth
black & gargoyles: keepers of the night
calling out   security has been breached
*

we are not evil.
I hear your heart   waxing
& waning like lemon drops on the tongue.
*

I missed you when we were gone.
You kept the dog   the house
the rabbit
*

as the doctor elsewhere scraped
a bladder & sutured
a lapsing seam.
*

We are not lemon drops or snowflakes
dissipating creatures we hang on
fiercely we hang on.
*

The drummer is loud   within you
high in the mountains
as the fern is an x-ray of war & peace
*

& Darth calls from doom
as the butterfly too calls from sight.

Miracles of homeless street

In the first miracle laughter was skinned   like mood
is skinned   through fat & muscle
down to the very bone.

In the second miracle he threw red over the canvass
with wicks of yellow   the orchard
closed in upon itself.

In the third miracle someone built a playground
for the homeless   hurriedly through storms of thunder
& hail the size of thumb prints.

In the fourth miracle there was no miracle
beyond two people seated in chairs facing each other
as one faces down void.

In the fifth miracle she laughed & was told not to laugh
she was told her humor had no substance
she wept in the bathroom for laughter was her cradle.

In the final miracle she could see through all futures
she could see how futures ended   she had a sense
that language is simply another separation from God.

Miracles of Neon Street

In the first miracle they departed church   built a circle
within the pine grove where needles clustered over red
mosses & they worshipped   by laughing hard.

In the second miracle she & her brother walked up
through the trees   talked about God & neon & why
buildings were unnecessary expression of human faith.

In the third miracle she & her brother played
throwing fragments of leaves in one another's hair
as the Dog Governor watched.

In the fourth miracle Governor was found by the
roadside   the girl sat with the abandoned   body
the spirit-forsaken body   stroking the January-rigid
muscles beneath the thick shepherd fur.

In the fifth miracle all walls were meant as toys placed in
the red toy chest gathered as a menagerie to arrange on
the windowsill when she so desired.

In the final miracle death had been confronted &
defeated   death had been defeated
as Freud said could not be done.

Miracles of Panama

She is going away   I am already sleepy. My body
collapses in upon itself
like a tortoiseshell beneath the gravity of seas.
    *

We didn't think we could have children.
The adoption agencies charged   thousands for an
infant from Korea or China.
    *

They asked   strange questions.
How much do you weigh. What paintings hang
over your walls.   Do you place hooks there.
    *

I went to Panama & arrived home
to an apartment that smelled of trees & rivers.
Soon I was pregnant.
    *

Frozen chocolate yogurt.
The food of the saints.
Carrot bread.
    *

I was no saint.
I am already sleepy   collapsing   afraid.
She is going away.

Miracles of the feral: Street of Bridges

We find ourselves in one another's wounds
feral wounds   like cats in the hills   lean
& hungry yet able to fend for themselves.
*

The skyline is like that:
looking upon its own wilderness as one looks close
in the mirror at the wounds of one's own eyes.
*

Is history nothing
but a furrow of our own making?   The old woman finds
passage in dire circumstance   her pianist hands
trembling
*

& forges onward like the Mother in the Sound of Music
singing into the window
when the colored film goes black on white.
*

We help one another   make bridges of our very bodies
straighten our spines that the vertebrae
will not trip any traveler.
*

I miss you.   But you were right
when you departed: was it death or wisdom that took
you far into the hollows of Brooklyn, without sound?
*

The insects form their own raiment
as they gather over the wound   still bleeding
even after the pain is finite   & all is clear.

Miracles of the Sea of Cortez

The humpback whale the scientists chance upon
appears dead   then blows a great noise   the waters
burst   *I am still here!!*
*

She is tangled in fishermen's wire
her fins pinned against her body   she cannot breathe
her great tail wrapped massively   dragged down
like a great root
*

rendered worthless.
They cut her free   it takes hours   wire piles
upon the boat's deck   men work around its villainy
*

Freed Valentina performs the sacred dance
of humpback whales   in the near distance following
the boat   the proximity of angels.
*

Doors open in the sky   doors open in the human heart
I am weeping.   I remember you saying
See that great humpback whale purpling the sky: it was
years before our daughter was born.
*

I read about a man   just let out of prison
the prison of Afghanistan
blinded by a blast of ancient shrapnel
*

& think how lucky we are
to have waters   fluent in parts of this world:
to afford the small efforts   of freedom.

Miracles of the Marina

Smells like oil
blue fish belly up on the Susquehanna River
dead still moving   in the houseboat's wake.
*

Liturgy is   a personal thing
formed of curses of eyes on the swirling stream of
bourbon over the deck.
*

There was no human death.   Passengers simply
vanished. Disappeared
like Chilean political prisoners.
*

The smell of gasoline
strident as summer sun   as the cigarette
smoke linked   in barbed wire chains.

Miracles of the Street of Few Words

Kayaking   or directing the ribbed canoe
she felt the crises pass as water trees pass
from light to shadow.
*

She had lain on her bed   a strange room
hearing barn owls beyond the sill
calling, calling.
*

Waiting   biting her upper lip
waiting   clenching her lower body
as if the maggots gather.
*

Joy is the mantra.   Too much laughter
that one is shushed in the movie theatre
watching a film   about magic horses.
*

Water trees ride the crests of time
as canoe or kayak   ride whitewater
in the axis of due storm.
*

I am a woman of few words
I shall not speak for her. Last night she lay sleepless
eating the ceiling pores   as one eats windows
*

in order to not be afraid
of departure. Essential departure
essential hello.

Miracles of the Street of Moth Echoes & Freaks,
a dream

In the first miracle she found herself on the Street of
Freaks eating mounded mint ice cream of a man she did
not love   riding a wagon of stolen guerilla books into
town.

In the second miracle her tongue was flayed
a cobra's tongue echoing   as the moth echoes against
pavement's verity & night.

In the third miracle pink intestines of Jesus spilled over
the frozen earth
with the innards of rabbits   & hungry   she ate of
them as of the trail snails leave when escaping
the wrath of the more eager insect.

In the fourth miracle the sands turned black the
intestines charred
all things were not true miracles   were rather the
magical legerdemain we form   & are formed by.

In the fifth miracle she found her name on the inner leaf
of a manuscript of sketches   yet had not signed it
herself: it had been rendered calligraphy by a choir of
oaks on the other side of the street.

In the final miracle all were released from the brick
asylum
the event of the encroaching world war
leaders feigned was not war   at once declared as
archived atoms fell & blue   missiles took flight.

Miracles of the Street without Vultures

There are no vultures
we thought we saw them circling
it was only the yellow haze of leaves departing the trees
for water's lack
*
Exiting this town
will be an exit from biography
will be an exit from the friends I adore.
*
He is alert in his hospital bed
we were freaked-out, creeped-out
we saw the vultures circling.
*
There are no hairy vultures.
Be prepared for anything   a friend says
we are.
*
We find a small Japanese restaurant
in the niche of an off-line mall
& eat fish & rice   & feel vigorous, until
*
the sudden thunder storm
forces us off the road   the road from my childhood:
forces us to no avail.

Miracles of Whisper Street (for my stepfather)

Whispers are manifest when we die. I believe you will
Be whole again.   Sweet gravel in the mouth to choke
Upon.   Words make no sense.
*

I see a brave front.   I see love.   I see years
In small caramels   laughter in stories of doors.
*

Yet unlike dogs   in the front yard humping.
The birds whisper.   This is somebody's bedroom the
Snow is gone
*

Yet we hear it crunch beneath our sneakers as its
Memory diffuses   I cannot wait to see you again.
*

What else is there to say?   All things are not   dusk
Draws back its face I see a rigorous disfigurement
I see a brave front
*

Miracles of streets of too many doors
Joy in a parallel world.

Miracles on Chico Road

In the first miracle it snowed on Easter: the dog ate the
rabbit in the center of the living room floor the white
carpet   was cleaned over night so the child remained
unaware.

In the second miracle` the child's imaginary playmate
named Chico went off to college & the child began
talking to herself alone by the bright green dumpster.

In the third miracle Chico became the name of a
restaurant   the character's name in a series of stories
or movies of fishermen & suns like Hemingway's Nick.

In the fourth miracle the fake moonlight
became more than her parents' orgasm on the stripped
bed moans walked in upon as one walks in upon horses.

In the final miracle all secrets closed eyelids to rest
there were no more secrets beyond the taste of the
vodka hidden in a brown paper bag under the sink.

Miracles on Court Street

In the first miracle the child pushed her fist through a
wall of glass   & there was blood they drove to the
emergency room   like swirling sirens like alto shrills
released from the conch song   aperture.

In the second miracle the emergency room played the
trial   of a woman who had allegedly murdered her two
year old child   placing duct tape over the pink, pink
mouth: they looked   away.

In the third miracle they waited three hours in a small
green-curtained chamber   as photographs wait in
a locket   the father answered when they telephoned
home   he was caring for the rabbit-hole white rabbit.

In the fourth miracle the doctor arrived from Ghana
with kindness he gauged no sutures were necessary
only butterfly strips of glue   & they laughed over his
story of putting his hand through a window   to acquire
his sister's pink, pink lollypop   when he was a boy.

In the fifth miracle the child spoke to the mother loudly all
the way home in order to keep her awake   while
driving   spoke loudly not accusing   for each was
tethered by imperfections by tantrums of just fallen rain.

In the final miracle the father was waiting as cartoons
played   X-Men & Avengers & the mother saw the
broken glass had not been cleared the mother sighed
resignedly & went to sleep   with guilt's bloodhounds
wailing.

Miracles on Forgotten Street (for Van)

The first miracle lay in the realization that scars are
meant to be kissed & tongued   as the rain bears down
on the tree-line   beyond the burnt down barn.

The second miracle lay in hearing stories of   Panama
& seeing the great red & blue colored strokes of the
fishing boats   collapse & inflate like lungs   over the
ancient   mansion's walls.

The third miracle lay in exchanging   yoga asanas for
drawing lessons early Saturday mornings   doing
the shoulder stand with a man still struck by   the wand
of first gestational   Alzheimer's.

The fourth miracle lay in finding cigars   in glass jars
from the second world war & opening the jars as if
fireflies   were contained within & lighting the tobacco
afire as if newly rolled.

The fifth miracle lay in the anti-miracle   of strangers
interfering in a friendship: of strangers interfering &
the yoga asanas ending   as she was learning to
sketch the sculpture of David's long muscles in charcoal.

The final miracle lay in saying goodbye without saying
goodbye   that wrench in the gut that fading silence
of rooms without corridor   rooms linked like elbows
rooms without end as memory never really ends.

Miracles on Glen Rock Street

Everything is a gift Jonny says.
Then again pain is a kind of contagion.   At the cookout
we ate cheeseburgers & discussed our thyroid levels &
played with little turtles
*

displaced from the Galapagos. We talked around the
pain.   Finally I scooched my chair over to one dear
friend: the urine is red I said the catheter bag is dark red.
*

Everything is a gift. We have brought joy
We have brought God
We have brought slices of cheesecake to keep in the
back pocket.
*

One contact lens ripped on the passage down.
At the swimming pool she tripped over the sidewalk &
her knee   a day later still reeks blood so the insects
gather.   (O yes that's me.)
*

The shade is beautiful
the shadows are lovely.   Saxophone blue. Is pain able
to be   shared like chocolates the box of chocolates
*

each wasted by trying to see what flavor it is?
I am far from neither life nor death
Karma's trying to tell you something   my daughter
says
*

as we leave the hospital.
Today she will get her first kiss from a boy who looks like
Frodo.   & the dog Piper gets meat for dinner.
*

That's never the case at home.
It's all a gift Jonny says. Truly
the water tastes like sun.

Miracles on Harpeth Knoll Road

In the first miracle
was the taste of the sixth beer when she was twelve &
the weight of ninety pounds.

In the next miracle
a fox was run over from the waist down
& flies on his hindquarters laid maggots even as he
lived.

In the third miracle
Big Foot was glimpsed as the girl spun round & round
before the bathroom mirror exclaiming Bloody Mary.

In the fourth miracle
the canoe was dragged ashore in the axis of a hurricane
& two children were rescued from the elements by a
drunkard   wrapped in blankets & fed tinned
sardines.

In the final miracle
the glass box vibrated like a grave & even world leaders
guilty of vast carnage were granted redemption.

Miracles on Market Street: the unraveling

In the first miracle she found a job she could tether
taking care of kids with Downs Syndrome   a girl
named Lucy pushed her into a velveteen pond.

In the second miracle the car's engine caught on fire
an olive camouflage Dodge a poof of smoke on the
highway as the iron vultures circled overhead.

In the third miracle she gave notice on her apartment &
where she moved there was a man
who had no sense of boundary.

In the fourth miracle eating became an impossibility she
was locked in a cellar come nighttime to piss
in an iron pot.

In the fifth miracle there was nothing to say she stood in
a room & the Man swiveled in his chair & pointed at her
& said   it must be hard dealing with that.

The final miracle embraced the voices jagged of
unraveling   at the hospital they examined her brain
with dyes & daggers & found something in the blood an
imbalance   without measure.

Miracles on Raleigh Drive

In the first miracle
she looked at the engagement ring & gasped
he threw it out the car window

In the second miracle
two cats fought outside the bedroom window
only one of the cats had claws

In the third miracle
he departed & was not missed
as most people do not miss the trials of winter

In the final miracle the children realized what evil means.

Miracles on River Street

The first miracle lay in living by the river   the moon
looping itself peeling our very bodies   until we were
immune to all disfigurement by virtue of orange light.

The second miracle spooled itself like streets around our
organs   until the ribcage was an unnecessary
embellishment   the streets held us intact with crack-
house jargon & brownstone mirrors.

The third miracle lay in   our exchanging our eyes
for hands   in exchanging the light for the darkness we
touched like the blind well & good   & not like cripples.

The fourth miracle took our hands as children take
hands in the convenience store seeking milk as candy &
we walked with the miracle   as if it was flesh & blood.

The fifth miracle immolated itself   called itself love in
the name of butchery & we swam like doves in the dirty
river   by the green   laundromat thin our feathers
plastered down, down.

The final miracle lay in the resurrection not of a body
but of a life: who saved us from ourselves but one
another   who saved us from the fire-pits of ourselves.

Miracles on the Street of Judgment

In the first miracle we were seated in the vet's waiting
room   talking & a beautiful dog came in dragging his
hindquarters   & we laughed thinking it was just
apprehension until we realized   the body was giving
way.

In the second miracle two people were strangers to one
another   living in the same family it took years & years
of condemnation before the younger said   I should
have asked you to walk me down the aisle.

In the third miracle streetlights flickered like tears over
her wet face & the mother did not telephone when she
should have telephoned   when she should have
expressed need.

In the fourth miracle the house on Wyndham Drive
echoed corridor on corridor great judges with their
gavels   on the cornice with singing black doves.

In the fifth miracle all who knew how to love emerged
from the underground railroad with its places for hiding &
for flight & came   to one place singing.

In the final miracle the body did not betray
the body did not give way   nobody lay in their hospital
bed   scared shitless watching the streetlamps flicker
like closing-in stars.

Miracles on Tri-Hill Drive

The first miracle
lay in having a new father
& the shiny yellow wreathes on the garage door.

The second miracle
rested in learning disappointment
in a way that refutes being written about.

The third miracle
resided in learning that the child is mother of the man.

The last miracle
prompted the child to come home not as a prodigal
as a human being.

Miracles on Wyndham Drive

In the first miracle red wine changed to water
& hummingbird hearts   unfastened from their feathers
pounced upon   like hands by the anaconda.

The second miracle resided in bringing a baby home
her long blue eyes bathing in the night in the memory of
day the bassinette laced with thick wedged violet ribbon.

(We do research as we go he says.
What are the common miracles I ask
raising the dead he says; water changed to wine; healing
the leprosy.
Can he take my voices I say; merge them as one.)

The third miracle resided in the cat pissing its body away
given insulin on a daily basis as he walked the threshold
mewing in retrospective as newborn rainbows mew.

In the fourth miracle laughter rose as smoke once rose
people ceased looking in the mirror
echoes curled like silhouettes against the snowy
avalanching mountain.

In the fifth & final miracle people left unsaid what did not
need saying   that is the stuff of forgiveness the stuff
of arriving to the cliffside   stones of peaches taken
from their orchard eyes.

IV. Prologue: alternatives to death

Miracles from the Gila Monster

It takes a nightmare to make me fly
Not even a jet could carry my weight   the cargo
of the dead & the living, each.

In the quicksand, sinking
listening to the rhythm of sucking noises
against the pattern of my ribs
Jesus walked away from me, laughing.

The Gila Monsters remain
when the electric bulbs flare
as if a spirited tombstone has entered the room.

My God, why did I leave it all unsaid?
At least he loved me, despite
each act of terror to the contrary.

I tell my mother: driving at night bothers me also,
the headlights in the rearview mirror
the headlights coming at me.   Difficult
to discern each from each   the future from the past.

Spend the night I tell her.
They have big beds, nearly coffins,
your feet won't dangle over the earth's lovely red edge.

Miracle of the Author's Bio

Circles cleaved like coconut shells
the milk of the fruit trembling.

I have blue eyes, not brown.
In this country I do not stand out
against the riptide. I have seen madness

I have seen violence
but I have seen much much love.
I have seen people saving other people at their own
deficit.

I have ridden the backs of hawks
as well as the backs of angels. Did I know, were they
fallen

or risen? No. I clutched the throat,
I felt the heave of the scapula beneath me, as the wind
tore through flesh that was or was not real.

Ah the milk was sweet.
Tadpoles flashed black in the inky creek.

The tree house was filled with a surplus of children
hiding from the closet's monster.
The wind was filled with song.

Trauma walked on its back, scuttling like a crab
along the sea.

What can I say. There was love much love.
There was the bruise's adrenaline, there was the red of
the fall:
there was much love.

Bonnie (2012) (sketch based on Jones photograph)
by Carolyn Srygley-Moore

Photographer, Brigit Srygley-Moore, 2012

Carolyn Srygley-Moore was born in York, Pennsylvania. She graduated, with awards, from the Johns Hopkins University in Baltimore.

Carolyn has been published by numerous reviews and anthologies. Most recently here work has appeared in Bone Orchard Poetry, Up the Staircase and Thus Spoke the Earth, a Haitian anthology.
Carolyn is also a poet activist for Real Stories Gallery Foundation, www.real.stories.gallery.com.

She has been nominated for the Pushcart and Best of the Web. Carolyn lives in Upstate New York with her husband and daughter.

Unified (2012) by Carolyn Srygley-Moore

www.ingramcontent.com/pod-product-compliance
Lightning Source LLC
Chambersburg PA
CBHW072356090426
42741CB00012B/3052